CCSS **Genre** Realistic Fic

Essential Question
In what ways can you help your community?

STANDING
GUARD

by Paul Mason
illustrated by Harriet Bailey

Chapter 1 Trash on the Beach

Ruby pulled herself through the ocean with strong, steady strokes, her arms and legs tingling in the cold water. She stopped to wave at her mom, who was standing on the shore.

Ruby then plunged beneath the surface. Suddenly she opened her eyes in horror. Something wide and clear had wrapped itself around her leg—it felt like a jellyfish!

Ruby clawed for the surface, expecting to be stung, but then she realized it was a plastic bag. "Who threw their trash into the ocean?" she thought. She snatched at the bag and swam for the shore.

"Good swim?" asked her mom. Ruby shivered and showed her the soggy bag. Her mom shook her head in dismay. "I remember when this beach used to be pristine," she said.

Ruby suddenly noticed rusty old cans, pieces of wrapper, and even the odd shoe scattered around. How come she'd never noticed the trash before?

Ruby looked around for a trash can. She noticed one at the northern end of the beach near the sand dunes, next to a sign that said "CAUTION: BIRDS NESTING."

As she walked up to it, she observed a man holding a clipboard and examining the sand. When Ruby approached him, the man swung around.

"It's a bird's nest," he said, answering her question before she could ask it. "Yesterday it had two healthy eggs in it, but not anymore."

Ruby crouched down in the sand, where she glimpsed a tiny, shallow indent in the sand like a bowl. It looked as if a shoe had flattened it. Inside, there were small fragments of shattered eggshell.

3

Ruby's heart dropped. "What kind of bird's eggs were they?" she asked.

"Piping plover. They breed here during the nesting season," the man said. "The species is endangered, and I work for an organization that's trying to protect them."

Ruby dropped the plastic bag in the trash can. "I'm impressed that you walked all the way here to use the trash can," he said.

Ruby shrugged. "It wasn't that difficult."

"It shows you care, and that's what matters. I'm Shane, the volunteer coordinator for Friends of the Piping Plover," he said, showing Ruby his badge. "We need more volunteers during the nesting season. Would you like to help?"

"What would I have to do?"

"Keep people away from the birds' nesting areas and keep the locals informed about the birds. You'd have to ask your mom or dad to accompany you though."

Ruby looked down at the shattered eggs again. "I'll ask my mom and dad," she said.

That night at dinner, Ruby's dad wasn't enthusiastic about bird sitting. "You know it's difficult for me to get around the sand on my crutches," he said. "The beach just isn't my favorite place, and your mom sometimes has to work weekends."

He noticed the disappointed expression on Ruby's face. "What's so special about these birds anyway?"

"They're an endangered species, Dad. I went online and found out that they nest on the beach, and people don't look out for them or care about them. I really want to help."

Ruby's mom agreed. "She's right. The beach isn't like it was when we were kids, Jack."

"And you're certain you really want to do this?" Ruby's dad asked, raising an eyebrow. Ruby could see he was softening.

"Come on, Dad. It'll be fun."

Ruby's dad smiled. "Then I guess we're going bird sitting! I'll give that volunteer coordinator a call."

That weekend, Ruby and her dad met up with Shane at the area of the beach assigned to them. Shane gave them each a "Friends of the Piping Plover" T-shirt and badges to wear with their names on them. He also provided them with a pair of binoculars and some brochures. "The brochures have information about the piping plover so people can learn about them," he said. "Knowledge is power, as they say."

Shane led them toward the dunes. "Now, after last week's incident, we've posted some more signs and roped off the area."

"That should be effective in keeping people out," said Ruby's dad, reading one of the signs.

"You'd be surprised," Shane muttered.

Shane was right. Even with the warning signs, people still attempted to put down their chairs or towels in the nesting area, and Ruby and her dad had to repeatedly ask them to move on. Fortunately, most people were pleasant about it once they understood why.

They also had to deal with some people who let their dogs off their leashes near the nesting area. Twice, Ruby's dad had to direct people away from the nesting area by waving and calling out to them.

By late afternoon, most of the town's residents had returned home. The beach became pretty quiet, and Ruby and her father had a chance to relax.

Ruby's dad peered through the binoculars across the dunes. "Hey, Ruby, check out these plovers," he said, handing her the binoculars.

Ruby stared through the lenses at a pair of small, sand-colored birds. They stood still, gingerly peering over the sand. They had distinctive black rings around their necks and another black line above their eyes, like a long eyebrow. Then suddenly the pair took off, sprinting across the sand—just a short burst of movement—then they stopped. They reminded Ruby of a child's toy, and they looked just as fragile.

"Those sure are lively little birds," Ruby's dad said with a laugh. "It feels good, doesn't it, knowing they're safe while we're here."

"Standing guard," she replied grinning.

Chapter 3 Night Shift

The next week, Shane called Ruby's dad.
"I realize you're new volunteers and I'm hesitant to take advantage of your generosity, but two of our volunteers are sick. Would you and Ruby be available to do the night shift this Saturday?" he asked.
"I'd do it myself, but I have to go out of town."

Ruby's dad thought about staying out all night on the dunes. "Yes, I guess we can do it," he said slowly. "There are some old sleeping bags around here someplace."

Shane sighed with relief. "Thanks a million, Jack."

Ruby's dad hung up the phone and smiled at Ruby. "Pack your bags," he said. "We're going camping."

On Saturday, Ruby assembled and packed everything they would need. She gathered food and water, a couple of powerful flashlights, some beach chairs, sleeping bags, and their warmest jackets.

As he watched Ruby rushing around excitedly, her dad had to admit that he was looking forward to it. After a long week at the office, it would be a welcome relief to camp out under the stars.

When they arrived at the beach, the afternoon sun was already lengthening the shadows of the dunes along the sand. The afternoon volunteers who were finishing their shift on the beach were ready to head home.

"It hasn't been too bad today," said one of the women. "There are still a few people lingering down by the picnic area, though."

"Yes, we heard them on our way in. I sure hope they don't keep playing that music all night," Ruby's dad said, nodding down the beach toward the faint thump of music.

"You have a good shift, now," replied the other woman as she turned to leave. As Ruby watched the two women wander down the sand, she couldn't help feeling a little jittery. She and her dad were alone on the beach. There was nothing but dunes behind them and waves crashing hard on the shore in front of them.

Ruby's dad unfolded his chair, lowered himself down, and began rummaging around in his bag. "I've got some homemade chocolate-chip cookies with our names on them," he said with a grin.

Ruby dragged her chair close to his. As they ate, they watched the surf rolling in over the sand.

Ruby's dad was quiet for a moment. "I haven't told you how grateful I am, Ruby," he said.

Ruby was surprised. "Grateful for what?"

"For you being so mature and insisting we get involved. It was the right thing to do."

Ruby could feel herself blush. "Thanks, Dad," she said softly.

"This certainly is a beautiful spot," Ruby's dad concluded, gazing out over the water. "One thing you can say about those plovers—when it comes to choosing a place to lay their eggs, they have excellent taste."

Out of the darkness came the revving noise of a car, which sounded as if it was at the starting line of a race. The noise ripped through the night air like a chainsaw.

Ruby picked out a car's headlights shining brightly at the far end of the beach. She assumed they came from an ATV about to race along the sand.

The driver released the brake, and soon Ruby could see an ATV speeding around the beach, its headlights flickering this way and that, as it leaped over the dunes. Above the noise of the engine, she heard people from the picnic area whooping and hollering as they cheered on the driver.

"Just when we were enjoying the peace and quiet, someone has to roar around tearing up the sand," Ruby's dad grumbled.

The ATV stopped for a moment, and Ruby thought she could hear voices. She guessed that they were taking turns driving the vehicle. Then, once again the whine of the engine caught on the wind, and the ATV screamed back down the beach. This time it was heading straight toward them and directly toward the nesting birds!

Ruby's dad reached for his crutches and pulled himself to his feet. "That driver is coming right at us!" he said urgently.

Ruby gasped. "Maybe he'll turn around," she said.

Chapter 4 Stopping Traffic

The ATV didn't turn around, and instead, it seemed to speed up, blasting toward them.

"Ruby, grab our flashlights out of the duffel bag!" Ruby's dad shouted. He couldn't keep the worry out of his voice as he headed quickly down the dune. "We've got to stop that ATV!"

Ruby ripped through the bag, her clumsy fingers struggling. At last she located the flashlights and flicked them both on, strong, bright beams lighting up the sand. Ruby ran down to the flat sand where her father was standing and handed him a flashlight.

The ATV showed no signs of slowing down. It was as if the driver hadn't seen them. Now Ruby and her dad began waving the flashlights back and forth, shining the powerful beams in the path of the oncoming driver, hoping to hear his engine slow down.

The ATV got nearer and nearer, closing in on the nesting area. Then, at last, there was a whine of gears and the driver began slowing down. The ATV rolled toward them and the engine finally cut out.

The driver swung his leg over the side of the ATV and approached them, unsnapping his helmet. "What's up?" he asked. "Is there something wrong?"

"I'll tell you what's wrong," Ruby's dad replied. "We've got some very rare birds nesting in those dunes behind us. Tires and birds' eggs just don't mix." Ruby could hear the steel in his voice.

Ruby stood beside him, shoulder to shoulder, and she swallowed hard. "They're called piping plovers," she heard herself saying, "and they come here every spring to breed." She was half expecting the man to snicker at her.

Instead, the man looked up at the dunes. "Really? My friends and I drive down this beach all the time. We had no idea there's a nesting area here."

"Well now that you know, maybe you should drive someplace else," Ruby's dad pointed out calmly.

"Yes, I guess we should," the young man nodded. "Sorry about the noise. I'll make sure we stay away from this end of the beach in future."

"Much appreciated," said Ruby's dad.

Ruby and her dad watched as the young man climbed onto his ATV and drove away cautiously, taking care not to let the engine growl too much.

"That was a bit of excitement," Ruby's dad said and then he sighed in relief. "We stood our ground, though."

"The plover's ground, you mean," Ruby said with a chuckle.

The following week, Ruby stood on the beach staring through her binoculars. Three new chicks, their feathers still fluffy, were already up and running. She watched the little birds as they tagged along after their parents, picking at the sand.

"Change over!" Shane called out as he came to join them. "I'd like you to meet a new volunteer."

Walking up the dune was the driver of the ATV from the weekend. "Hey, guys," he said, looking sheepish. "Lucky for me this group isn't too selective to have me as a volunteer. I love this beach, and getting involved just seemed like the thing to do."

"That's great!" Ruby said as she handed him the binoculars. "Here, take a peek at your new friends."

"Wow," said the young man as he stared through the lenses. "You did a good job the other night keeping these guys safe."

"We certainly did," thought Ruby as she and her dad headed for home. "We really did."

Respond to Reading

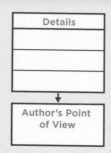

Use important details from *Standing Guard* to summarize the story. Your graphic organizer may help you.

Details

↓

Author's Point of View

Text Evidence

1. How can you tell that *Standing Guard* is realistic fiction? **GENRE**

2. Is this story told by a first-person or a third-person narrator? Use examples from the text to tell about the narrator's point of view. **POINT OF VIEW**

3. What are *brochures* on page 6? Use clues in the paragraph to figure out the meaning. **DEFINITIONS AND RESTATEMENTS**

4. Write about how the narrator's point of view helped you understand the characters in this selection. **WRITE ABOUT READING**

Compare Texts

Read about a community program that helps children.

THE GREAT BIG BIRTHDAY BASH

Have you ever wanted to make a difference in your community? Volunteers can make a big difference, and they often benefit from the experience, too. This is what teenager Sean Nathan of Shreveport, Louisiana, discovered.

While volunteering at Providence House, a homeless shelter, eighth-grader Sean discovered how difficult life is for children who don't have a home.

Sean was shocked to find out that one of the kids never celebrated his birthday. Sean decided to act, and with the help of the staff at the shelter, he and his brother Neil hosted the first ever Providence House Birthday Bash.

Former First Lady Laura Bush congratulates Mark Landry, 17 (center), and Sean Nathan, 14 (right), on being named the top two youth volunteers in Louisiana for 2009.

Sean and Neil now hold birthday parties for the children at Providence House. There are pizzas, cakes, music, games, and, of course, presents.

To raise money for the parties, the boys give music concerts. They also ask restaurants to give them a discount on the pizzas they serve the kids. Sometimes the pizzas are even donated.

Sean believes all their hard work is worth it. "It gives me great satisfaction to watch the kids have parties," he said.

WHAT CAN YOU DO?

There are many ways you can make a difference in your community. You can:

- visit an elderly family member

- pick up trash

- hold a bake sale and give the money to charity

- volunteer at an animal shelter

- clean out your closet or bookshelf and donate items to a charity

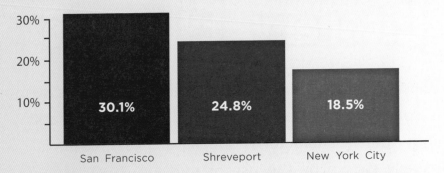

Volunteer Rate

San Francisco	Shreveport	New York City
30.1%	24.8%	18.5%

This graph compares the percentage of volunteers in Shreveport with the percentage of volunteers in New York City and San Francisco. How do you think your area would compare?

Sean's story shows how ordinary kids can make a big difference to other people's lives. What's more, Sean and his brother are not alone. In their city of Shreveport, Louisiana, nearly a quarter of the residents do volunteer work. That's an average of nearly 60,000 people helping out each year.

Volunteers do many kinds of jobs, from working with people to caring for animals. There are many different organizations or charities in every community. What kind of volunteer work would you like to do?

Make Connections

How does Sean's work help the community of Shreveport? ESSENTIAL QUESTION

What do *Standing Guard* and *The Great Big Birthday Bash* tell you about why people get involved with community projects? TEXT TO TEXT

Focus on
Literary Elements

Dialogue Writers have several ways to show us who is speaking and how they sound. Quotation marks show that a character is speaking. The speaker is usually shown by the use of *said* and their name.

Read and Find In this sentence, you know right away that Ruby's mom is speaking:
"Good swim?" asked her mom. (page 2)

Using the context of a sentence can help you figure out who is speaking:
"Thanks a million, Jack." (page 8)
This sentence is not attributed, but we assume it's Shane speaking because it follows from his previous speech.

Your Turn

Copy this chart. With a partner, look for examples in the story of the different ways that dialogue is written. Fill in the chart with the examples you find.

Dialogue	Example
Using *said*	
Using the sentence context	
Using a verb other than *said*